Guinness World Records' Fastest Banjo Player

TODD TAYLOR PRESENTS

"PICKIN' OVER THE SPEED LIMIT"

THE CLASSIC ROCK N' BLUE TABLATURE BOOK

Table of Contents

ISBN 978-1-57424-262-1
SAN 683-8022

CENTERSTREAM®

Copyright © 2011 CENTERSTREAM Publishing, LLC
P.O. Box 17878 - Anaheim Hills, CA 92817
www.centerstream-usa.com

Foreword
by Todd Taylor

I PERSONALLY WOULD LIKE TO THANK ALL of my wonderful fans and banjo pickers around the world for your great support. Many of you have asked me for a Todd Taylor banjo book of my tablatures of these songs. Finally I'm happy to say here it is! As many of you know the banjo she's been my whole life. The banjo is a happy joyful instrument that will always make you smile! I was just six years old when I started playing. I remember my parents had taken me to Disney World in Florida and we were sailing on the Tom Sawyer riverboat and suddenly I saw a guy strumming a banjo. What was that? I was instantly mesmerized. On the way home I was so hooked, I knew I just had to have one. My mom bought me my first banjo from the JC Penney Catalog and it was a Kay. After I started playing I discovered Earl Scrugg's incredible playing and he is the one great banjoist who became my mentor and hero. Years later with my solo career really blossoming through many recordings and tour's, I fell ill and was diagnosed with an incurable terminal rare muscular disease. When the doctor's all told me I wouldn't survive and gave me just six months to live, I knew I had to prove them wrong. MY GREATEST moment in life is definitely beating this disease back and playing my banjo on the MDA Telethon- to try to help other people who also live with muscle disorders. I've been real lucky to survive and to enjoy sharing the stage with legends such as Bill Monroe, Roy Acuff and many more. And I must say having this disorder wasn't gonna stop me because once I decided it, I practiced everyday for a year to compete and successfully set the world record for the Guinness Fastest Banjo Player. It's been the ultimate dream realized. And it's the number one BEST thing in my life too because in my heart I know I'm doing this for all handicapped and disabled people everywhere. "Don't ever give up on your dreams in life cause if I can do it - I know we all can make it happen." I've really enjoyed sharing MY own style of Banjo playing for everyone all of these years, and I really love to play rock and roll, great bluegrass and much more. The power of this instrument is always so amazing to me. It is with great honor and gratitude for life, that I say 'YOU my fans mean the world to me!' Thank you for all of the support through the years, and there will be many more to come. So, with that being said, God bless you all and I hope to see you on down the road sometime.

—Todd Taylor

Special thanks to John Rogers, David Pericone, Ken Marler, Steve Thorpe RIP, Tim Hutchins, Lynne Robin Green, Rick Dee's, Jack Roper, Kimberly Kelly, Gary Williams, Chris at the Break, and to the MDA Muscular Dystrophy Association, and The Regional Hospice House Of South Carolina.

Dedication
by Todd Taylor

I WOULD LIKE TO DEDICATE THIS BOOK TO The MDA Jerry Lewis Telethon, my Mom and Dad, James Taylor and Nancy Taylor, *thanks for buying me my first banjo,* and also Sheb Wooley, Thornton Cline, and Lynne Robin Green, *thanks for all your dedication, hard work and guidance. YOU are all the best!* And thanks to GHS Strings, Stelling Banjos, Mike Moody, Gracie Muldoon, and the good Lord for giving me the talent to play the banjo. I'm grateful that God gave me this great gift and with every accomplishment that I've enjoyed *"I dedicate this gift to everyone who lives with or faces insurmountable struggle in their lives that they don't feel they can overcome." I'm living proof YOU CAN accomplish anything you want to do in life!*

Producer's Message

WHEN I FIRST CONCEIVED THE IDEA of producing a banjo tablature book of Todd Taylor's original songs along with the incredible banjo arrangements of the rock songs he plays here, I knew THIS would be a really extraordinary project. I am very inspired by Todd's life story seeing this incredibly gifted young musician and survivor who's beat all the odds to overcome an incurable rare disease, and who challenged himself with the greatest test to become The Guinness World Record's Fastest Banjo Player in the World. Here's a young man who's part angel I'm sure and who refuses to say I can't. He's a role model and a personal example of strength, faith, hard work, and mastering your craft. He's EVERYMAN'S biggest dream realized! I know that Todd's incredible career is destined for helping others with his talent and indestructible personal strength. He's living the simple truth - *"When God gives you a gift YOU USE IT."* He has dedicated HIS life and that gift to doing good work continuing to inspire people all over the world. *It's a real pleasure and a great honor to be a part of this very special book....*

—*Lynne Robin Green*

Credits: Songbook Concept, Coordination and Production by Lynne Robin Green www.LWBHmusicpublishers.com. All Banjo Song Notations By Bruce West. Graphic design and layout by Beyond Tomatoes www.BeyondTomatoes.com. Specially produced for and with extra appreciation to Ron Middlebrook, Centerstream Publishing.

Biography
by Lynne Robin Green

TODD TAYLOR IS A FOUR-TIME GRAMMY NOMINEE and The "Guinness World Record Holder for Fastest Banjo Player." He was the first person in history to establish and set the world record and he is the current record holder. He played Arthur Smith's Feuding Banjos, aka Dueling Banjos, at 210 beats per minute and his record has never been broken. The Guinness Organization has retired Todd's record and it now lives forever in the history books. In 1974 Todd originally founded The Taylor Twins along with James Taylor. The Taylor Twins toured the circuit with legends in Bluegrass such as Bill Monroe, Carl Story, Jim & Jesse, and more including memorable performances at The Grand Ole Opry and more. Todd went on to perform with Roy Acuff on The Nashville Network, and Nashville On The Road Show with many major country acts. Todd became The First Banjo Player in history to take the banjo to the Rock-N-Roll crowd worldwide on his album Todd Taylor - Something's Different which charted and lead to his performing his remake of the classic rock song "Free Bird" aka -Taylor's Freebird on Rick Dee's Rock and Roll Top 40 Countdown Show (his original tablature of FREE BIRD is featured in this book now available for the first time). A Grammy Nominated Recording Artist, Todd was nominated two years in a row for his "Blazing Bluegrass Banjo CD" (artist nomination) and for Todd Taylor -Taylor Made Bluegrass. Ultimately with a total of 24 Grammy category nominations throughout the years 2004-2005-2006-2008 and since those days nothing is stopping Todd from sharing his great playing with bluegrass, rock and country music fans everywhere.

Discography of Todd Taylor

Todd Taylor - Something Different - 1987/reissued 1999
A Bluegrass Christmas - 1989
Beethoven's Nightmare - Todd Taylor - 1991
Todd Taylor - Silent Night - 1991
Merry Christmas Vol 1 - 1991
The All American Composers Library
Americana Vol 2 - Traditional Music of The U.S. - 1991
Todd Taylor Patriotic Medley - 1994
Sweet Liberty Volume 1 - released 1998
Sweet Liberty Volume 2 - released 1999
Todd Taylor - Fastride - 2000
Taylor's Christmas - 2000
Todd Taylor - Blazing Bluegrass Banjo - 2003
Todd Taylor - Taylor Made - 2004
Todd Taylor - 3-Five-2005
Todd Taylor - Bringin It Home - 2008
Todd Taylor - The Best Of - 2009
Todd Taylor - Diversity - 2010

Magazines and print with feature articles about TODD TAYLOR include:
Banjo Newsletter, front cover article - 1984
Banjo Newsletter, front cover article - 2005
Country Weekly, article Blazing Banjo - 2007
Bluegrass Music Profiles, front cover article - 2004
Guinness World Book Of Records - 2009 Issue
Bluegrass Unlimited, reviews
Guinness World Records Calendar
BBE Focus Magazine world wide "the country's greatest banjo player"
Breaking and Entering, Film Documentary about Guinness World Records (Todd and his music performance featured).
The Nashville Network/CMT Country Music Television/ABC TV New York
CBS Evening News with Katie Couric/CBS WORLD WIDE
With Jerry Lewis The MDA Telethon/Stage 36-Hollywood
Fox Sports South with Jerry Adams

Fishing Country/John Fox's Outdoor Adventures on Fox Net ESPN
Family Net/Odyssey Network - Swans Place
World Wide Radio - Rick Dee's Weekly Top 40 Countdown featured Artist
Todd's Freebird and Stairway To Heaven/with Sheb Wooley At The Grand Ole Opry
Firefox Internet - Commercial spokesman - Todd Taylor Fastest Banjo commercial spot
Excedrin commercial - Performance
The Hunt Feature Film - Produced By Grey Fredrickson and Fritz Kertz's musical
performance in film.

Artists Todd Taylor has performed with or opened shows for include:
Bill Monroe, Carl Story, Leon Everette, Stella Parton, Johnny Paycheck, Jim & Jesse Jerry
Clower, Roy Acuff at The Grand Ole Opry and many more.

Endorsements:
Todd Taylor is endorsed by GHS Strings and Stelling Banjos.
Signature Banjos designed The Todd Taylor Gold Tone Signature Tree Of Life Banjo
in his honor.
The Music Link Recording King Banjos.

The Song Tablatures

All banjo arrangements created by Todd Taylor

CD Track List

1. 3-Five-N
2. Unleashed
3. The Race Is On
4. How Great Thou Art
5. Wayfaring Stranger
6. Six Gun's

Freebird

Words and Music by Allen Collins and Ronnie Van Zant

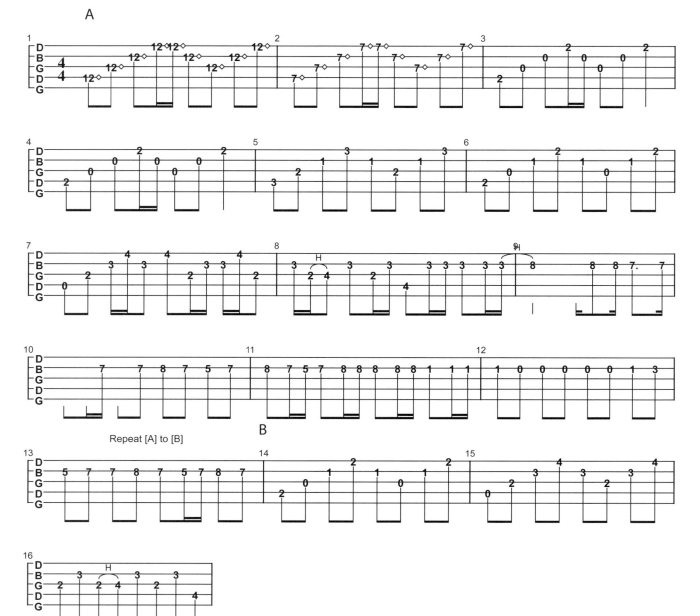

Repeat [A] to [B]

Dust in the Wind

Words and Music by Kerry Livgren

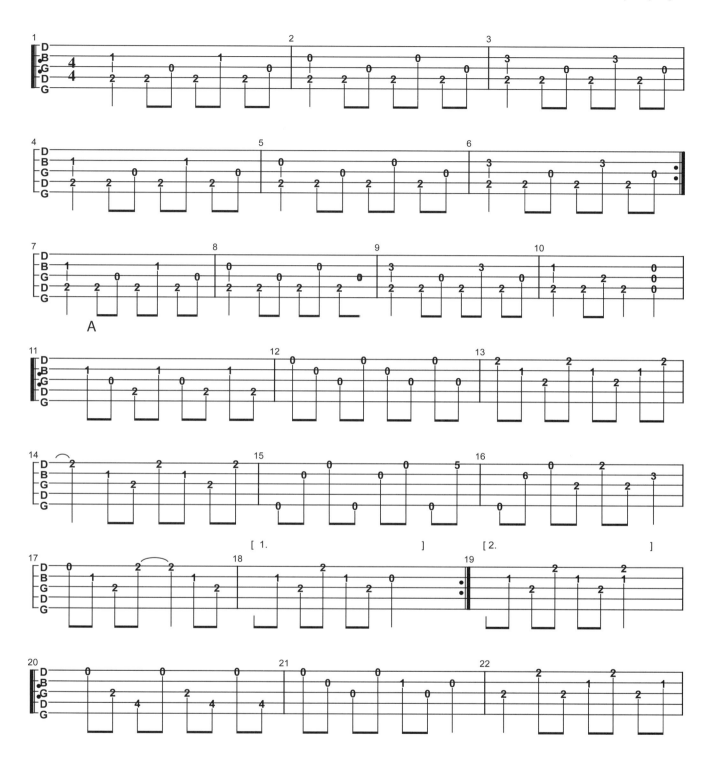

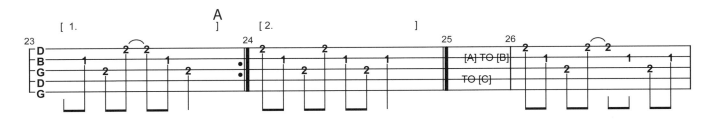

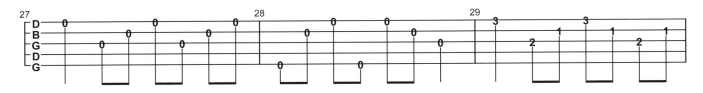

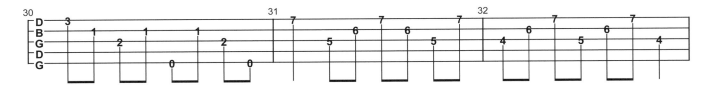

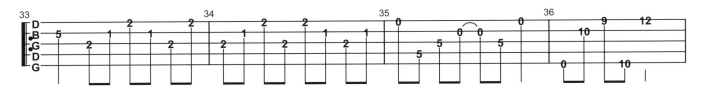

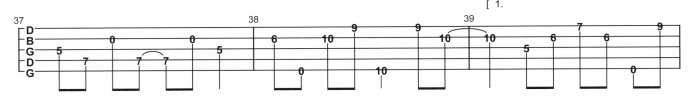

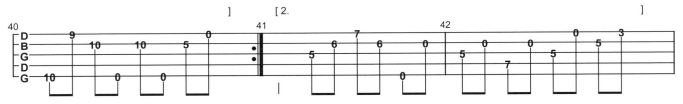

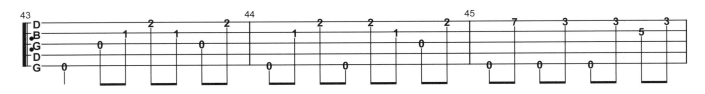

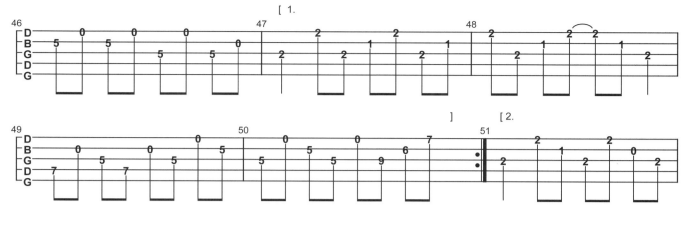

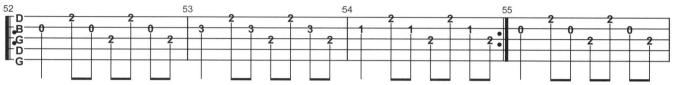

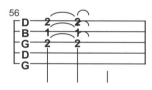

El Cumbachero

Words and Music by Rafael Hernandez

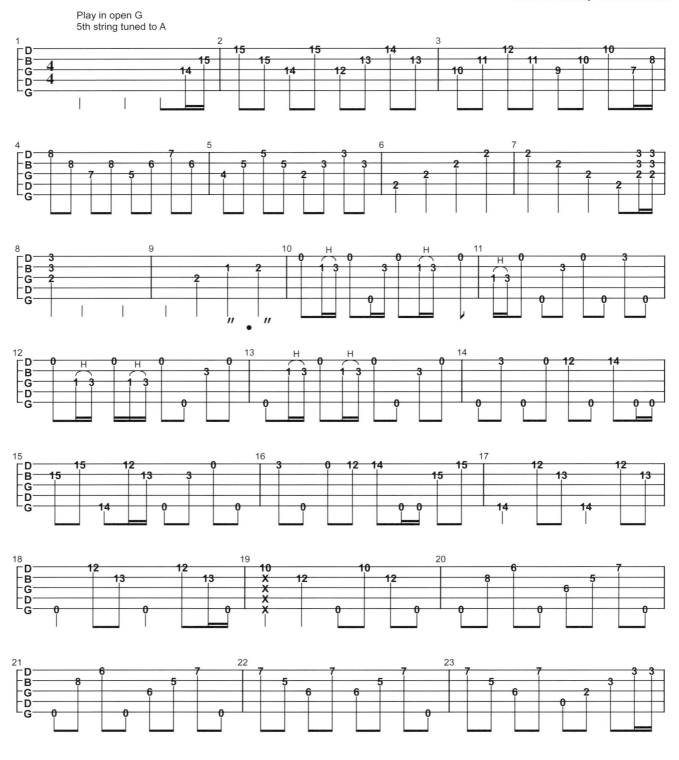

Page 1 / 2

12

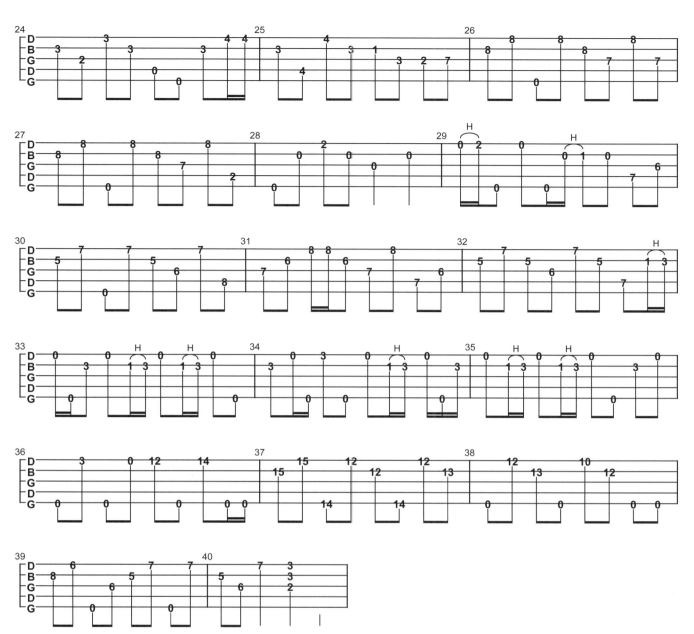

strum

3-Five-N

(todd taylor) ASCAP

Capo 4th fret
Play in B

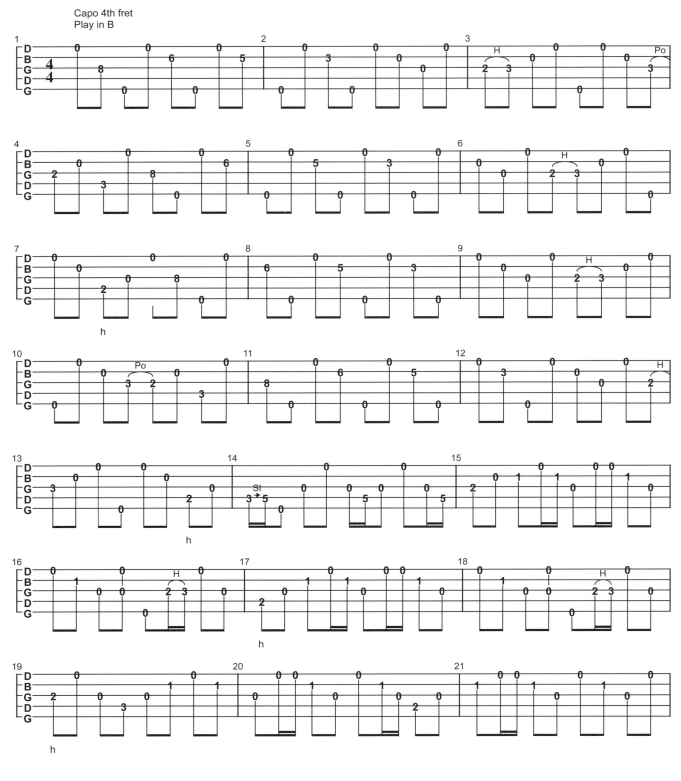

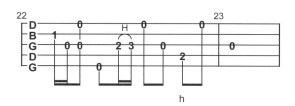

Page 2 / 2

15

Rocket Man

Words and Music by Elton John and Bernie Taupin

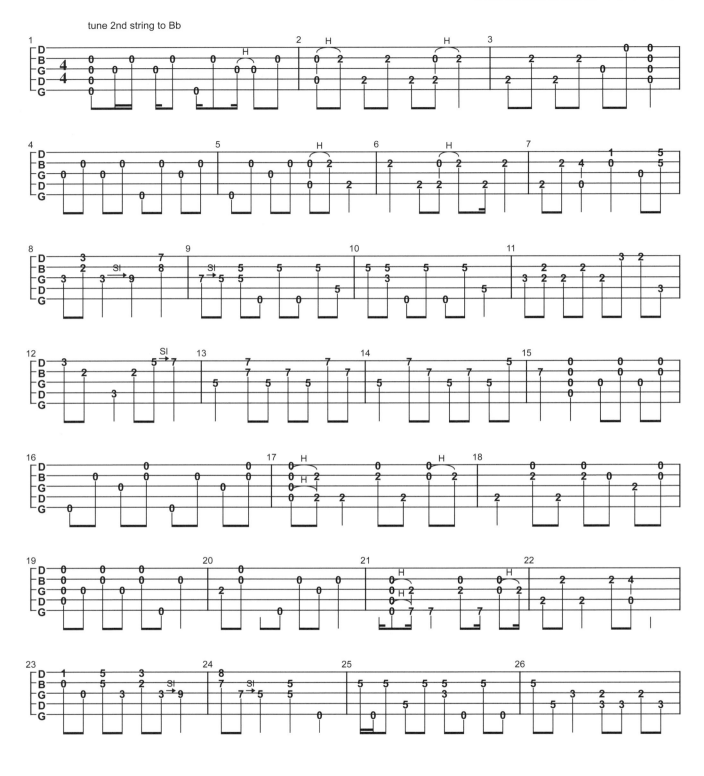

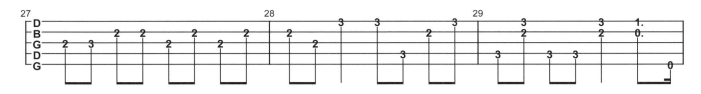

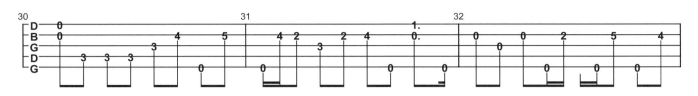

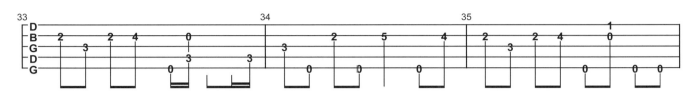

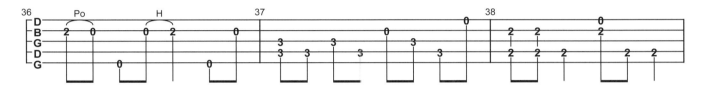

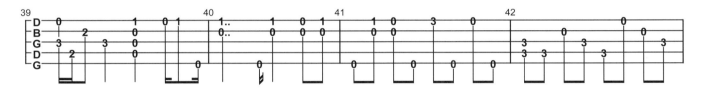

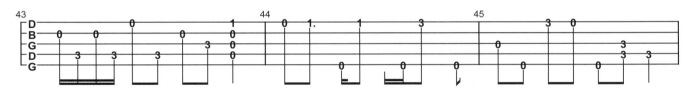

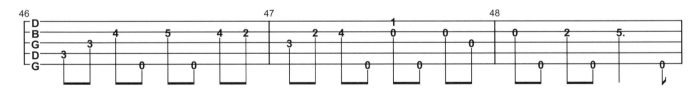

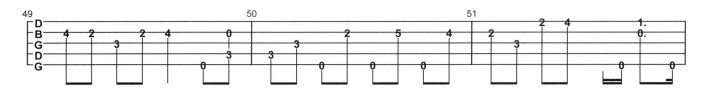

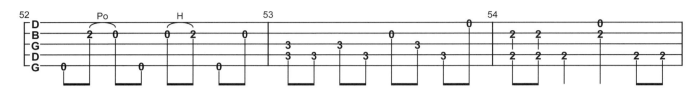

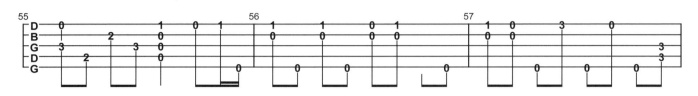

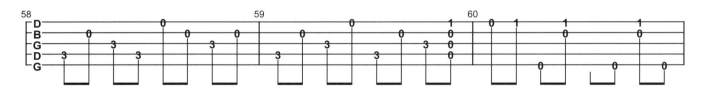

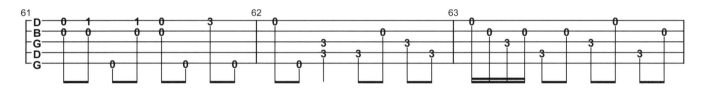

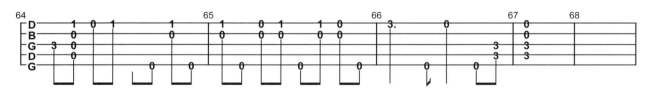

Page 3 / 3

18

Six Gun's

(todd taylor) ascap

Double C Tuning

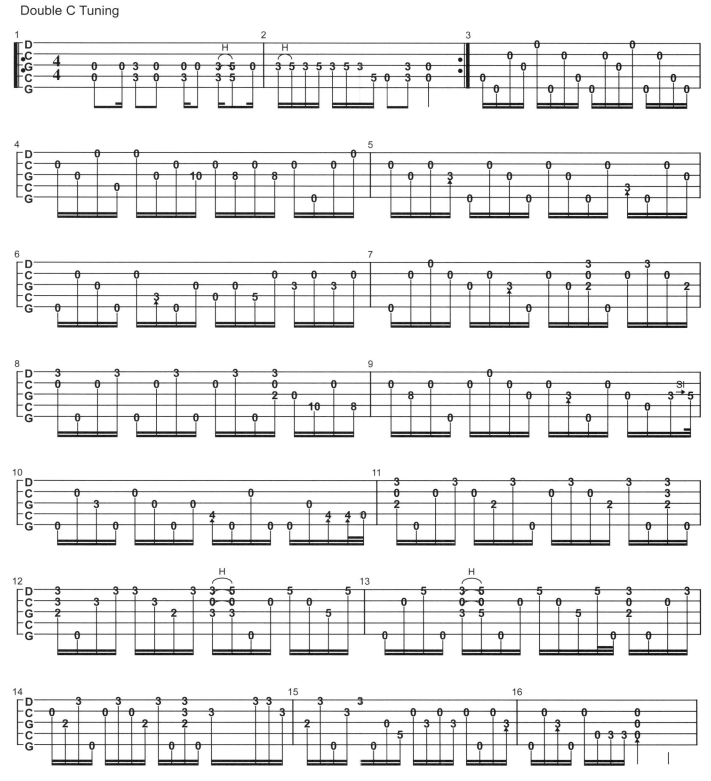

Unleashed

(todd taylor) ASCAP

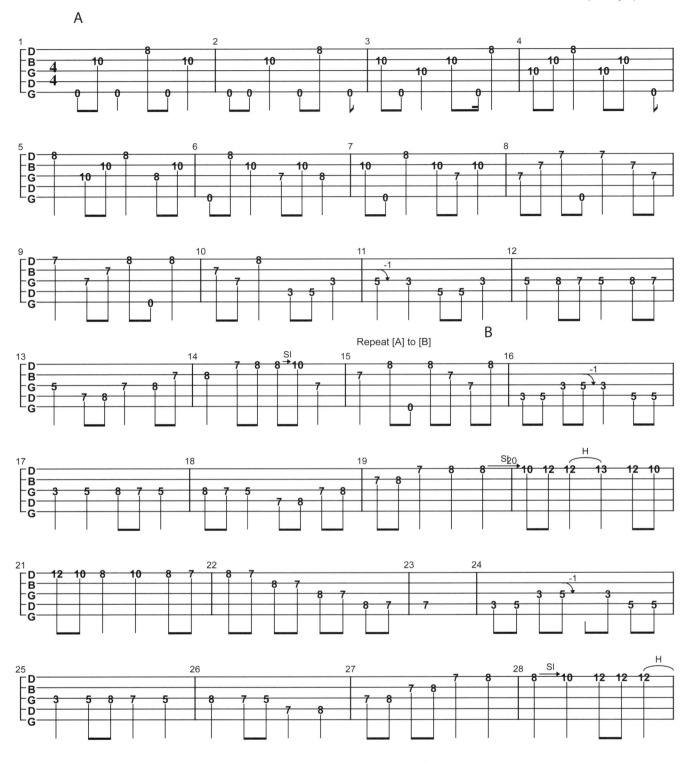

Repeat [A] to [B]

Page 1 / 2

20

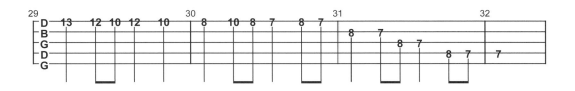

Norwegian Wood

Words and Music by John Lennon and Paul McCartney

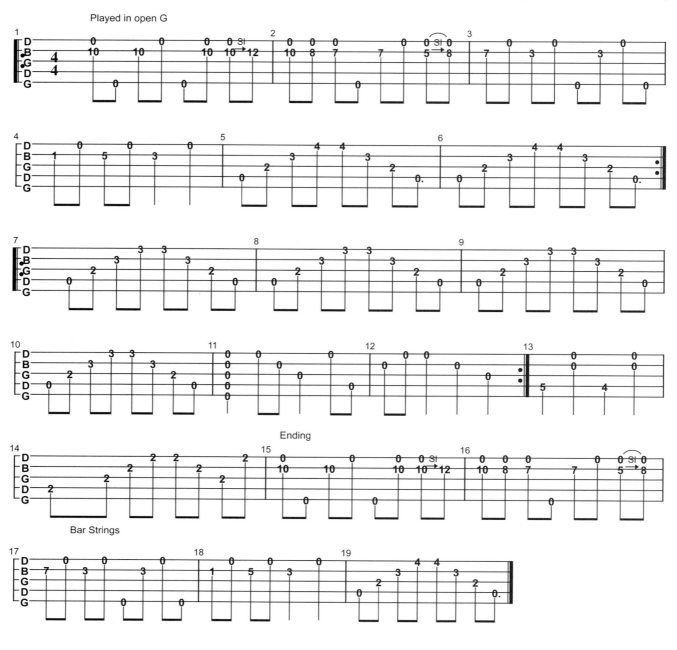

The Race Is On

(todd taylor) ASCAP

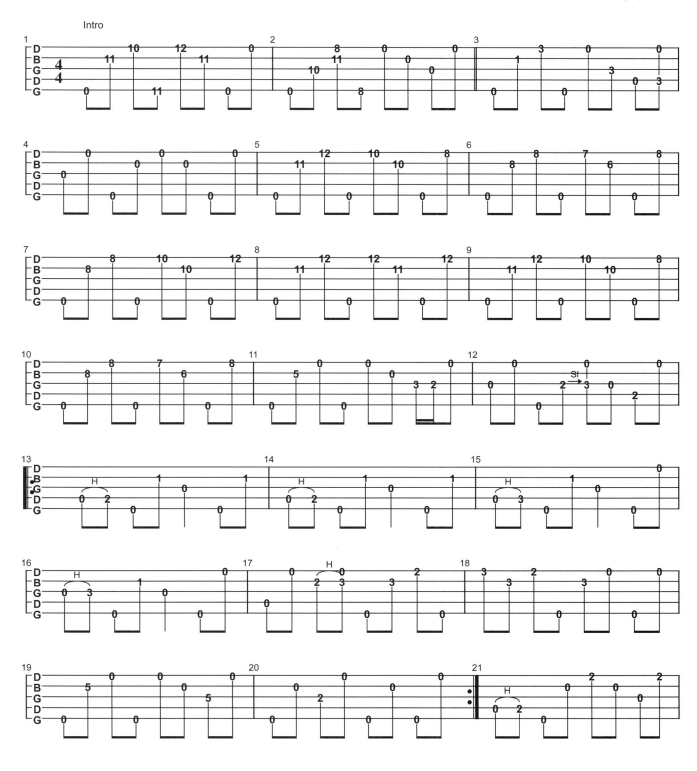

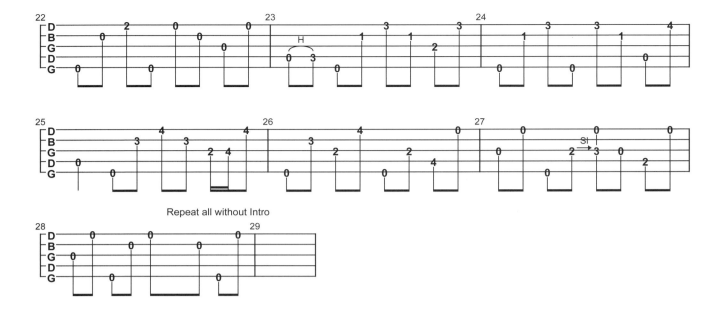

Repeat all without Intro

I Know A Little

Words and Music by Steve Earl Gaines

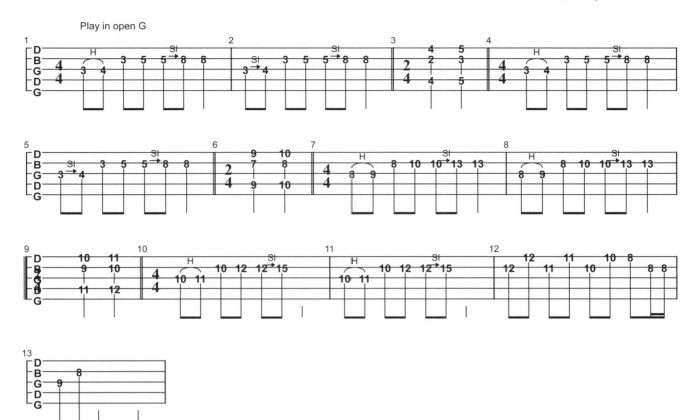

Play in open G

Yackety Sax

Words and Music by James Rich and Boots Randolph

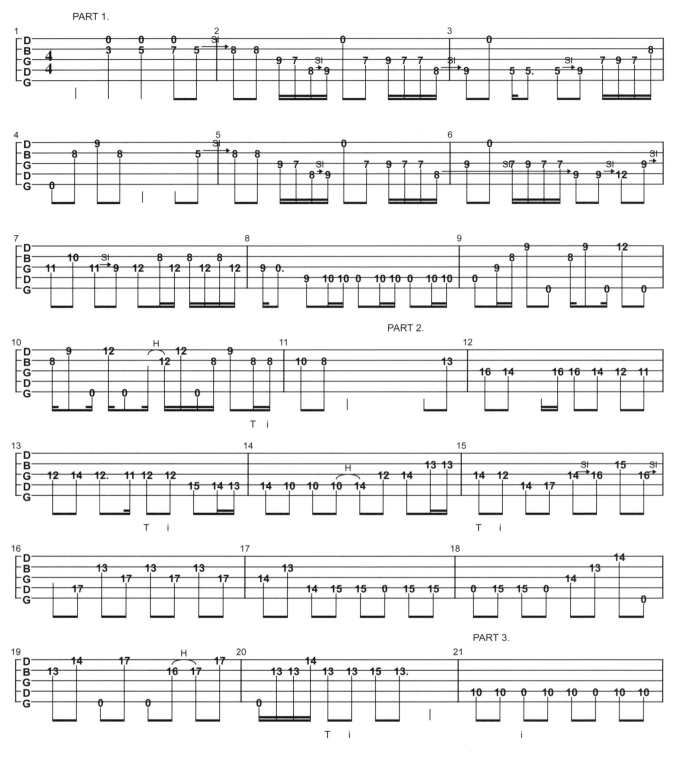

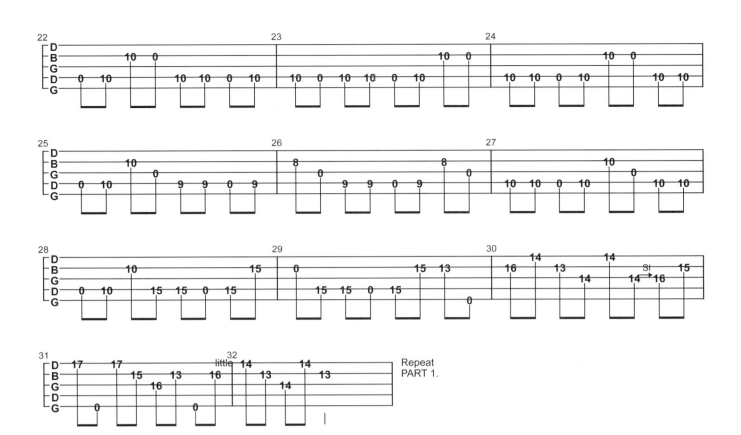

I Can't Stop Loving You

Words and Music by Don Gibson

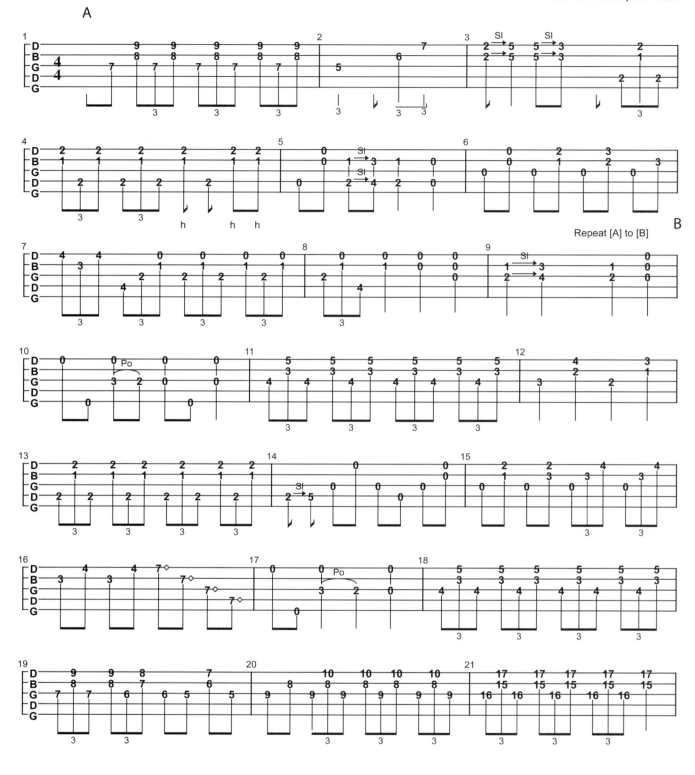

Page 1 / 2

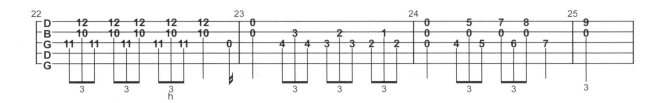

How Great Thou Art

(trad. arrgmt - taylor) ASCAP

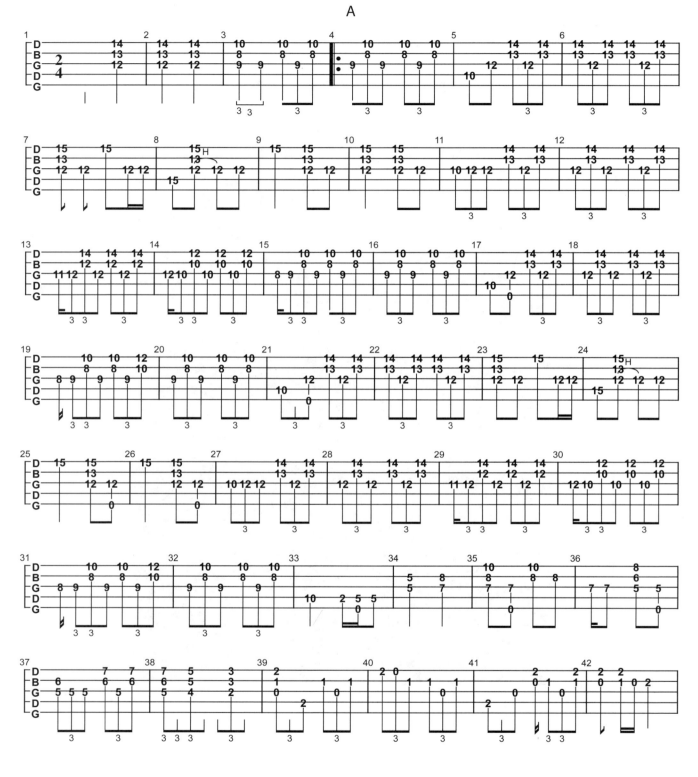

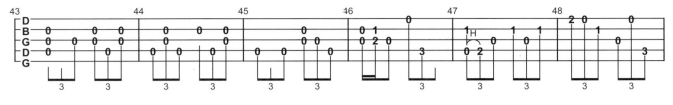

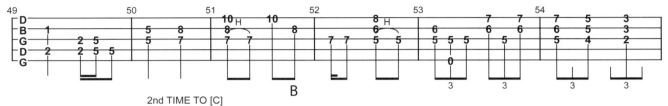

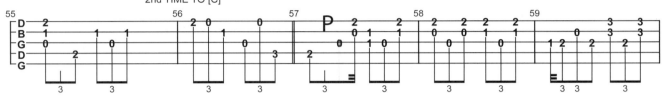

2nd TIME TO [C]

B

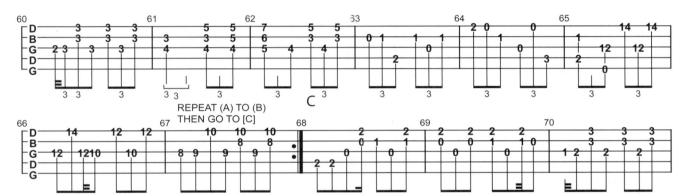

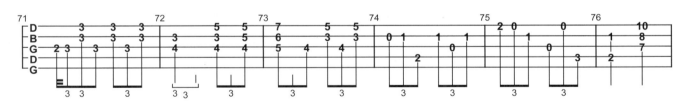

C

REPEAT (A) TO (B)
THEN GO TO [C]

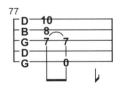

Wayfaring Stranger

(trad arrgmt -taylor) ASCAP

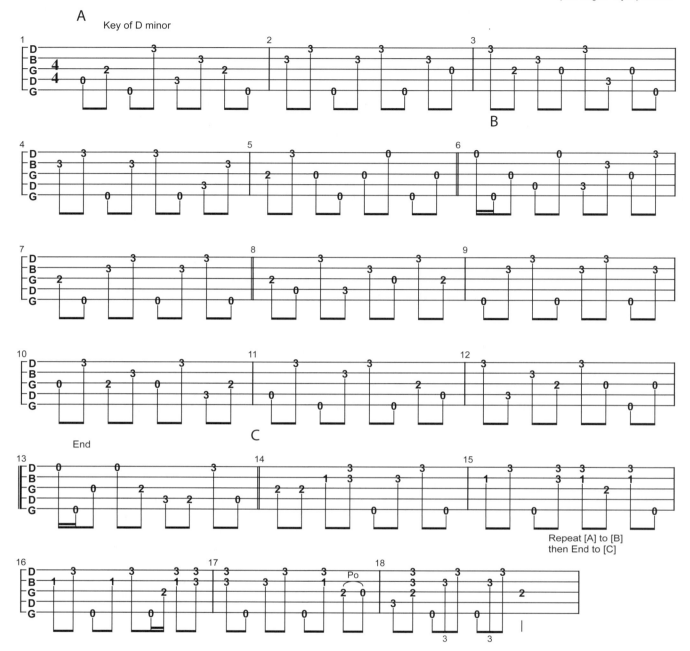

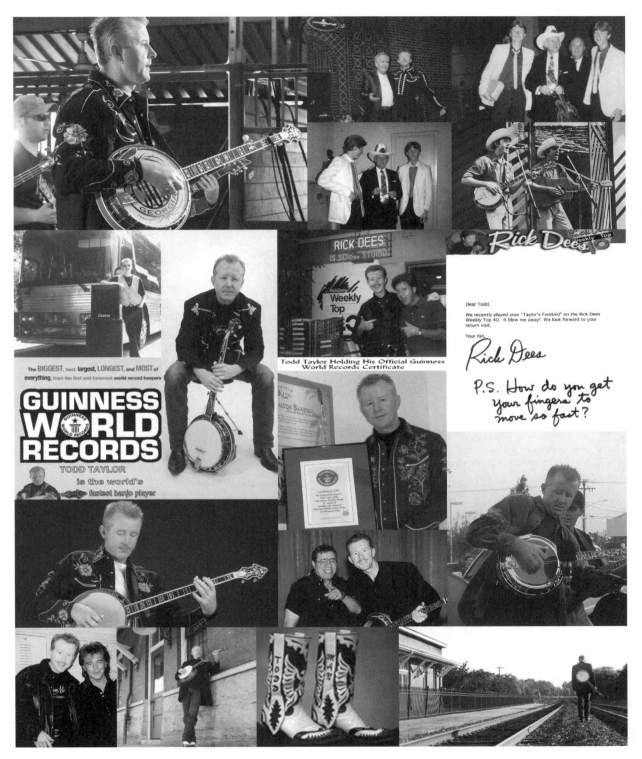

Highlights from Todd Taylor's career

*Top mid-right with Sheb Wooley, Taylor Twins with Roy Acuff,
Todd with Marty Stuart, and others.

BANJO   Centerstream Publishing   Centerstream@aol.com

5-STRING BANJO CHORDS
by Ron Middlebrook
The only chart showing the open and moveable chord positions. Explains the two main playing styles, bluegrass and clawhammer, and includes a fingerboard chart.
00000074 ....$2.95

5 STRING BANJO NATURAL STYLE
No Preservatives
by Ron Middlebrook
Now available with a helpful play-along CD, this great songbook for 5-string banjo pickers features 10 easy, 10 intermediate and 10 difficult arrangements of the most popular bluegrass banjo songs. This book/CD pack comes complete with a chord chart.
00000284 Book/CD Pack $17.95

CLASSICAL BANJO
40 Classical Works Arranged for the 5-String Banjo
by Kyle R. Datesman
40 works from the Renaissance and Elizabethan period presented in chordal and a more linear manner. Includes an informative introduction about the origins of the music and playing style.
00000179.................................$12.95

BEGINNING CLAWHAMMER BANJO
by Ken Perlman
Ken Perlman is one of the most celebrated clawhammer banjo stylists performing today. In this new DVD, he teaches how to play this exciting style, with ample close-ups and clear explanations of techniques such as: hand positions, chords, tunings, brush-thumb, single-string strokes, hammer-ons, pull-offs and slides. Songs include: Boatsman • Cripple Creek • Pretty Polly. Includes a transcription booklet. 60 minutes.
00000330 DVD $19.95

INTERMEDIATE CLAWHAMMER BANJO
by Ken Perlman
Picking up where *Beginning Clawhammer Banjo* leaves off, this DVD begins with a review of brush thumbing and the single-string stroke, then moves into specialized techniques such as: drop- and double-thumbing, single-string brush thumb, chords in double "C" tuning, and more. Tunes include: Country Waltz • Green Willis • Little Billie Wilson • Magpie • The Meeting of the Waters • Old Joe Clark • and more! Includes a transcription booklet. 60 minutes.
00000331 DVD $19.95

CLAWHAMMER STYLE BANJO
A Complete Guide for Beginning and Advanced Banjo Players
by Ken Perlman
This handbook covers basic right & left-hand positions, simple chords, and fundamental clawhammer techniques: the brush, the "bumm-titty" strum, pull-offs, and slides. There is also instruction on more complicated picking, double thumbing, quick slides, fretted pull-offs, harmonics, improvisation, and more. Includes over 40 fun-to-play banjo tunes.
00000118 Book Only $19.95
00000334 DVD $39.95

THE CLASSIC DOUGLAS DILLARD SONGBOOK OF 5-STRING BANJO TABLATURES
This long-awaited songbook contains exact transcriptions in banjo tablature that capture the unique playing style of Douglas Dillard. This fantastic collection includes all of his best-loved tunes, from "The Andy Griffith Show" to his solo banjo albums and his releases with The Doug Dillard Band. Features more than 20 tunes in G tuning, C tuning amd G modal tuning, including classics such as: Cripple Creek • Hickory Hollow • Jamboree • John Henry • Old Joe Clark • Buckin' Mule • and more. A must-have for all banjo players!
00000286 ....$19.95

THE EARLY MINSTREL BANJO
by Joe Weidlich
Featuring more than 65 classic songs, this interesting book teaches how to play the minstrel banjo like players who were part of various popular troupes in 1865. The book includes: a short history of the banjo, including the origins of the minstrel show; info on the construction of minstrel banjos, chapters on each of the seven major banjo methods published through the end of the Civil War; songs from each method in banjo tablature, many available for the first time; info on how to arrange songs for the minstrel banjo; a reference list of contemporary gut and nylon string gauges approximating historical banjo string tensions in common usage during the antebellum period (for those Civil War re-enactors who wish to achieve that old-time "minstrel banjo" sound); an extensive cross-reference list of minstrel banjo song titles found in the major antebellum banjo methods; and more. (266 pages)
00000325.................................$29.95

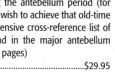

THE BANJO MUSIC OF TONY ELLIS
One of Bill Monroe's Bluegrass Boys in the 1960s, Tony Ellis is among the most renowned banjo players around. This superb book assembles songs from four highly acclaimed CDs – Dixie Banner, Farewell My Home, Quaker Girl and Sounds like Bluegrass to Me – capturing his unique two- and three-finger playing techniques in the bluegrass style in standard notation and tab.
00000326 ....$19.95

GOSPEL BANJO
arranged by Dennis Caplinger
Features 15 spiritual favorites, each arranged in 2 different keys for banjo. Includes: Amazing Grace • Crying Holy • I'll Fly Away • In the Sweet By and By • Just a Closer Walk with Thee • Life's Railway to Heaven • Nearer My God to Thee • Old Time Religion • Swing Low, Sweet Chariot • Wayfaring Stranger • Will the Circle Be Unbroken • more!
00000249 ....$12.95

MELODIC CLAWHAMMER BANJO
A Comprehensive Guide to Modern Clawhammer Banjo
by Ken Perlman
Ken Perlman, today's foremost player of the style, brings you this comprehensive guide to the melodic clawhammer. Over 50 tunes in clear tablature. Learn to play authentic versions of Appalachian fiddle tunes, string band tunes, New England hornpipes, Irish jigs, Scottish reels, and more. Includes arrangements by many important contemporary players, and chapters on basic and advanced techniques. Also features over 70 musical illustrations, plus historical notes, and period photos.
00000412 Book/CD Pack $19.95

MINSTREL BANJO – BRIGGS' BANJO INSTRUCTOR
by Joseph Weidlich
The Banjo Instructor by Tom Briggs, published in 1855, was the first complete method for banjo. It contained "many choice plantation melodies," "a rare collection of quaint old dances," and the "elementary principles of music." This edition is a reprinting of the original Briggs' Banjo Instructor, made up-to-date with modern explanations, tablature, and performance notes. It teaches how to hold the banjo, movements, chords, slurs and more, and includes 68 banjo solo songs that Briggs presumably learned directly from slaves.
00000221 ....$12.95

MORE MINSTREL BANJO
by Joseph Weidlich
This is the second book in a 3-part series of intabulations of music for the minstrel (Civil War-era) banjo. Adapted from Frank Converse's *Banjo Instructor, Without a Master* (published in New York in 1865), this book contains a choice collection of banjo solos, jigs, songs, reels, walk arounds, and more, progressively arranged and plainly explained, enabling players to become proficient banjoists. Thorough measure-by-measure explanations are provided for each of the songs, all of which are part of the traditional minstrel repertoire.
00000258 ....$12.95

The Competition

Those using
Centerstream
Books & DVDs